Financial Literacy Made Easy

CREDIT EDITION

By Kesha Oliver Robinson

Copyright © 2012 Kesha Oliver Robinson

All rights reserved. This book or any portion thereof may not be reproduced or used in any manner whatsoever without the express written permission of the publisher except for the use of brief quotations in a book review.

Printed in the United States of America

First Printing, 2017

ISBN-13: 978-1976253072

Dragonlife Publishing
P.O. Box 60663
Savannah, Georgia 31420

www.UnchainYourDragon.com

CONTENTS

Introduction	1
Knowledge Assessment 1	5
Information you Really Need to Know	13
Myths about Credit	17
Understanding Credit	25
Credit Report	45
Activity	52
To-Do List	54
Knowledge Assessment 2	56
Glossary	67

Kesha Oliver Robinson

ACKNOWLEDGEMENTS

First, I would like to thank everyone who has pre-ordered Financial Literacy Made Easy: Credit Edition and everyone who will purchase this book in the future. This book is dedicated to my community of Savannah, Georgia. I know you've made bad decisions based off of being miseducated and misinformed, but as long as you have breath in your body, you have a chance to do something different and get different results. I am a firm believer that if you learn something new that can help your community, it is your responsibility to go back and teach someone who doesn't know the same information. It is disrespectful, as a matter of fact, it's betrayal not to attempt to educate your brothers or sisters in need.

There are so many people who have been instrumental with the process of writing this book that I couldn't possibly name everyone. I would like to thank each one of my friends and family members who listened to my ideas and community resolutions day after day after day. Thank you Ms. Natarielle Powell, who is one of the best English professors in the world. I would not have been able to publish this

Kesha Oliver Robinson

book without you. Because you helped me edit and design the front and back cover, I was able to complete Financial Literacy Made Easy: Credit Edition in less than a year. Thank you for your encouragement, advice, skills, and friendship. Last, but not least, I would like to thank my husband, Mr. Robinson, and my teenagers, Kiana and Kevin, for being my rock. You are the reason my heart sings. Thank you, family, for being selfless and sharing your bomb.com wife and your bomb.com mama with the world.

Introduction

Congratulations! Welcome to the first step to obtaining financial literacy and wealth. Wealth? Yes, wealth. Knowledge is wealth, and hopefully, after you finish this credit book and activities, you will feel like you have an increase of understanding of credit and the knowledge necessary to make informed decisions about your credit goals.

What is financial literacy? I'm glad you asked. Financial literacy is a basic understanding of finances aka "Money." What does money have to do with credit? I'm glad you asked that too. Money has a very close relation to credit. Most people do not use money to make large purchases; they use credit. An excellent credit score can help you achieve financial goals like starting a business, purchasing a home, or purchasing an automobile.

We live in a world where money matters. Sometimes, you hear people talk about money, but they don't talk about credit. Credit is just as important as money.

Thank you for investing in me and most importantly thank you for investing in yourself! I decided to write this book because I care. Yes, I care about you although we've never met. I am a Community Leader, Educator, Power Speaker, Realtor and Serial Entrepreneur who loves her community and feels that not enough people give back to it. So instead of complaining, I've decide to do something!

When most people hear give back, they automatically assume that I am talking about money. Wrong! One of my favorite quotes is "Give a man a fish, and you will feed him for a day. Teach a man to fish, and you will feed him a lifetime!" So, if I give money but do not educate, I will have to give money daily. I would rather teach you how to fish. Let's learn how to fish here!

Why should I aspire to have good credit?

Because it will save you money!

A good credit score and report can save you over $200 monthly on a 30-year $100,000 mortgage by allowing you to obtain a loan at a lower interest rate.

Good Credit	Bad Credit
Interest Rate = 3.7%	Interest Rate = 7.25%
Monthly Payment $460	Monthly Payment $682.18

Amount Saved Each Month = $222
Amount Saved Over 30 Years = $80,000

Test your Knowledge

Let's see what you already know about credit and effective ways to build and rebuild it. Don't Google any answers; just answer the questions honestly. You will gain more knowledge throughout this book. After a quick recap, you will be able to revisit this assessment and see how much you've learned!

Part 1

True or False

1. Buy Here Pay Here accounts are some of the best accounts to rebuild your credit.

2. Equifax and Experian are two credit repair companies

3. A credit repair company can help you increase your credit score to 800.

4. Paying off your automobile loan can help me obtain good credit.

5. There are three major credit bureaus: Equifax, Transunion and Experian.

6. I can obtain good credit by making my monthly mortgage payments.

7. Student loan accounts do not report late payments.

Multiple Choice Questions

1. Credit is
   a.) money
   b.) an account
   c.) buy now pay later
   d.) a, b, & c

2. My _____ should stay below 25% of my credit limit to help increase my credit scores.
   a.) debt to income ratio
   b.) credit score
   c.) credit card balance
   d.) inquiries

3. There are _____ major credit reporting agencies.

   a.) two   c.) five

   b.) three   d.) one

4. What are inquiries?
   a.) new credit accounts

   b.) late payments

   c.) when a creditor looks at your credit report

   d.) derogatory accounts

5. You can order a **FREE** yearly credit report from
   a.) www.equifax.com
   b.) www.transunion.com
   c.) www.annualcreditreport.com
   d.) www.experian.com

6. If you are denied for a credit card, you may want to apply for a _____ card.
   a.) Master   c.) Visa

b.) Debit   d.) Secured

7. What is interest?
   a.) taxes
   b.) late payments
   c.) the amount of money you pay back to creditor
   d.) the amount of time it takes to pay back a loan

Part 2

True or False

1. If I am trying to build my credit, I should open a personal loan account.

2. An installment account is a contract that clearly states the date when the contact will close.

3. On-time payments will help me achieve an 800-credit score.

4. A 620-credit score is considered poor.

5. I must wait seven years after bankruptcy to purchase a home or automobile.

6. Bankruptcy accounts report monthly to all three credit bureaus.

7. A maxed-out credit card does not hurt my credit scores if I make my monthly payments on-time.

Multiple Choice Questions

1. An account with an end date is a (an)

    a.) revolving account

    b.) credit account

    c.) closed account

    d.) installment account

2. A relationship between a creditor and a customer that allows the customer to purchase items or services before payment is

    a.) credit

    b.) capital

    c.) a customer

    d.) interest

3. You are considered the _____, and the person or company lending you credit is the _____.

    a.) creditor, borrower

    b.) borrower, creditor

    c.) customer, borrower

    d.) borrower, bank

4. A _____ is a revolving account.

    a.) savings account

b.) installment card

c.) credit card

d.) checking account

5. Which score is considered good credit?

    a.) 610- 670   c.)760- 850

    b.) 611-below   d.) 680-759

6. Personal, automobile, and mortgage loans are _____.

    a.) installment accounts

    b.) credit accounts

    c.) bank accounts

    d.) revolving accounts.

Kesha Oliver Robinson

Information you REALLY Need to Know

According to the Fair and Accurate Credit Transactions Act ("FACT" Act), passed by Congress on November 22, 2003, consumers are allowed to obtain a free credit report every 12 months without paying any fees. You can request a copy of all three of your credit reports (Equifax, Experian and Transunion) by contacting www.annualcreditreport.com (1-800-322-8228), a centralized service for requesting a free annual credit report. Be mindful of these other online free credit report companies. You are entering your personal information, and you want to make sure it is a government-trusted website.

Negative information can impact your ability to get a loan, obtain a credit card, rent an apartment, etc. Incorrect information regarding your credit report can remain on your credit report for up to seven years. It is very important that you monitor your score and report for misinformation so it can be corrected as soon as possible, to minimize the damage done to your score and/or report. If the bureau is unresponsive, you can file a complaint with the Consumer Financial Protection Bureau (CFPB) at www.consumerfinance.gov.

Be careful not to accumulate unnecessary debt. The higher the amount of debt you have, the lower your credit score will be, and a new creditor will be less likely to lend you money and/or credit.

Credit reports contain the following information: personal identification information (including previous and current addresses, employment information, social security number); past and current credit card accounts (numbers and types of accounts that are past due and in good standing); loans and repayment history (including late payment history); mortgages; the numbers and types of inquiries made into your credit history; bankruptcies; child support payment history; and statements of disputes. The report does not contain the following: your credit score (paid for separately) and information about savings accounts, checking accounts, or other investments.

The information used on your credit report helps a new creditor determine whether or not the company is will to take a risk on you and lend you money and/or credit.

Myths about Credit

What is a myth? A myth is any invented story, idea, or concept also known as the untruth. Credit myths are dangerous, if you apply these ideas to your everyday living. It can possibly cause you to take several steps backwards and push you further away from your credit goals. Let's discuss a few common credit myths.

On-time payments will build my credit.

> *Credit myths are dangerous, if you apply these ideas to your everyday living.*

It depends on the type of account you are paying on. Every creditor who allows you to obtain a credit account with them is not created equal. You should fully understand each creditor's reporting standards before you open a new account.

If I pay my automobile off, I should have excellent credit.

Yes and No. If you made on-time payment you will have a good credit history, but an automobile loan is an installment account. See installment vs revolving account in

Understanding Credit for more details.

I pay my mortgage on time; I should have good credit.

Yes and No. If you made on-time payment you will have a good credit history but a mortgage loan is an installment account. See installment vs. revolving account for more details

Credit Repair companies give me good credit.

The goal of Credit Repair companies is to remove derogatory accounts off your credit report. Depending on how old the account is, it can increase your credit score. You must obtain a new credit card, make on-time payments, keep you balance 25% below you limit, and avoid maxing out your credit card after or while the credit repair company is removing derogatory accounts off your credit report.

I can't buy a home or automobile because I am in Bankruptcy.

Truth be told, it is easier to purchase a home in bankruptcy than if you wait until your bankruptcy is discharged. When you file for bankruptcy, all accounts that are on your bankruptcy case are no longer allowed to report to the credit agencies even if you are late. Translation- your bankruptcy accounts are frozen, so while you are rebuilding your credit the derogatory account are not affecting your scores. Sometime while in bankruptcy your score will be drop to zero or Not Scoreable because you do not have any open credit account being reported for 1 to 5 years. It is extremely easy to increase your credit score while in bankruptcy.

1. Obtain a secured credit card (a traditional credit card company will not approved you for an account while in bankruptcy)

2. Make on-time payments.

3. Keep secured credit card balance below 25%.

Personal loans can help build my credit score.

No! No! No! No! This is one of the most famous lies! Small loan companies have been deceiving borrowers for many years, their famous line is "Do you want to renew your loan? You always pay on time, renewing your loan will help build your credit score. Wrong!!! Wrong!!!! (Loud Buzzing Noise) Loans are reported as an installment loan. See Installments Vs Revolving Accounts in Understanding Credit for more details.

Early payments (before the actual due date) can help build my credit or increase my score.

Your creditor will only report once a month on the same day. Paying on your account early does not increase your credit score, nor does it provide early payment notations on your credit report. It's a good habit to train yourself to pay your bills early, but for the sake of rebuilding increasing your credit score and improving your credit report, early payments do not help.

Late payments do not really hurt my credit score.

Late payments and maxed out credit cards are the number one reason for lower scores. One late payment can decrease your score up to 100 points. It can take six or more months to recover those same 100 points you lost due to a late payment. Not only does a late payment decrease your credit score, but it can also cause a different credit account that is in good standings to decrease your credit limit because of a late payment on another account. For example if you have an ABC Credit account for $5,000 (in good standing), and your EFG Credit account $6,000 has a late payment, ABC Creditor may randomly check your credit report for late payment and maxed-out credit cards (it's legal and usually in the fine print that we don't read). Once ABC Creditor is made aware of the changes to your report, they can decrease your credit account to $1,000 because you are now considered as a bad risk.

Understanding Credit

Excellent	760- 850
Good	680- 759
Fair	611 – 679
Poor	610- below
No Score	No Credit

What is credit?

I'm glad you asked. Credit is basically trust. It is a relationship between a creditor and a customer that allows the customer to purchase items or services before payment, based on the trust that payment will be made in the future. In other words, buy now, I trust you to pay for the product later, whether it's an automobile, a home, boat, furniture, gas, etc.

There are three major Credit Bureaus: Equifax, Transunion and Experian.

Each credit score can range from 300-800, any score below 610 is considered low and any score above 680 is considered good. Why do you have three separate scores? Because each credit bureau reports an individual score using their own scoring system. It is possible to have a 400, 500, and 600 score at the same time.

You will not obtain a high credit score without making on-time payments to your credit account.

A credit account is any account that allowed you to purchase a product or service without paying the full balance. Example: If you purchase a home and you did not pay with cash, you used a mortgage loan. You made an agreement with the mortgagor to pay a mortgage (monthly payments) until your balance is paid in full. One late payment can reduce your credit score up to 100 points.

> **To obtain a high credit score, you will need to**
> - obtain a credit account that reports to all three credit bureaus every 30 days
> - keep your balance at 25% of your entire limit and
> - make on-time payments.

Longevity is a very important factor to consider when trying to become a member of the 700/ 800 club. (Good/ Excellent Credit).

Having a long-term credit account (3-5 years) will help you elevate your credit score, but it's not enough to just have an open account for 3 to 5 years. You should spend no more the 25% of your credit limit each month. It shows the creditor that you are a responsible credit account holder, and it reinforces the trust which would cause the creditor to increase your limit.

Creditor = Lender   Borrower = You

It is important to understand the roles of creditor and borrower before obtaining any credit account. When you are applying for credit, you are asking a business/entity to enter into a relationship with you based on trust (the Creditor will look at your credit history aka credit report). The role of the lender, also known as the creditor, is to assess if lending monies to the borrower is a risk the lender is willing to take based on the history of your credit report. If your creditor decides to take a risk and allow you to open an account with the company, your interest rate depends on your credit history and score.

(Interest – how much you are going to pay the company back for allowing you to buy now and pay later, translation: profit that the creditor will make off the borrower) The lower the credit score, the higher the interest rate (the more you pay back). The higher the credit score, the lower the interest rate (less money you pay back). The borrower role is simple: borrower money and/or credit, make monthly payment on time, and borrow money/credit again.

Installment Vs. Revolving Accounts

An installment account is an account that has a contract (binding agreement enforceable by law) with an established end date. For example, you borrow $100 from 123 Credit Company. The 123 Credit Company contract states that you agree to pay $25 a month for 7 months, if you do not make your payment and default on this agreement, 123 Credit Company can file a **judgment** against you and possibly garnish your employment paycheck.

Installment accounts will close once you make your last payment at the end of your contract agreement. This type of account will show a history, but is not the best method to take if you are trying to increase your credit score because once you make you last payment and the account is closed, your credit score will decrease.

A revolving account is an account that increases and decreases based on your on-time payments and balance. If you make on-time payments and keep low balances (below 25%), creditors will most likely increase your credit limit. Low balances demonstrate to creditors that you are a responsible credit card holder. A revolving account does not close when you make your last payment unlike an installment account. For example, if your balance is $10 and you made your last payment and your account balance is now $0 you still have an open account with 123 Credit Company, but if you have an installment account (Automobile, Personal Loan or Mortgage) and you make you last payment and your balance is $0, your account is closed forever, never to reopen.

If you want to open another personal or automobile loan, the creditor will open a new account for you with new account number, it doesn't matter if it is the same creditor.

Obtain a credit account that reports to all three credit bureaus every 30 days.

Let me let you in on a little secret; creditors

Financial Literacy Made Easy

have to pay a fee to report your monthly payments, so sometimes they do not report

> **Before you obtain a new credit account, always ask the creditor which credit bureaus it reports to and how often.**

to all three bureaus. What does this mean? I'm glad you asked. A creditor can save tons of money if they report to only one bureau or report once every 6 months instead of every 30 days. For example, if your Experian score was 400, Equifax 500, and Transunion 600, and your creditor only reported to Equifax, Equifax is the only score that will increase. But if you had an account that reports to all bureaus every 30 days, all scores will increase together, instead of moving around in a circle like musical chairs. An example of musical chairs is if your credit scores are 525 Experian, 550 Equifax, and 575 Transunion, and creditor Company ABC only reports to Experian because they have a small monthly fee, if you continue to have a good payment history with company ABC, it could increase your score up to 100 points in the matter of a year. Experian, which was your lowest score could leap in front of Transunion which was your highest score. Transunion could drop to your lowest score and Equifax could remain in the middle. So, in the matter of a year, because credit company ABC only reported to one bureau, your new scores could look like this: Experian 625, Equifax 550, and Transunion 500. So, although you made on-time payments for a year, your middle score would still be 550.

Credit limit and balance. Your credit limit is how much credit (money) the creditors loans you. Your Balance is how much you

spent.

If Company 123 gives you a credit limit of $500, and the salesperson tells you instead of paying cash you should charge $500 to you credit account, do you think this was a good idea? No, you just maxed out a credit account, therefore you could decrease you credit score up to100 points in 30 days. Do not panic we all have made uninformed credit decisions. But that's why I am here to help.

It is very important that your credit limit and your credit balance are never the same amount.

Rule of thumb: never spend more than 25 percent of your credit limit. For example, if your credit limit is $500, you should only spend $25 per $ 100 of your credit. This total is $125 out of the $500. If you go over your $125, don't panic; just work on paying your balance back down.

Can I Trust you?

This is the number one reason creditors deny new accounts. History dictates rather or not a creditor will give you an account. A credit account is saying I will give you my product or lend you money under the assumption that you will pay it back with interest in a timely manner. Trust is built. One of the reasons why a creditor will start you off with a $100 credit limit is to see if you are able to make on time payments on a small loan or credit limit. As you make on-time payments you will build trust and the company will increase your limit. If a creditor cannot trust you with $100, what makes you think this company will trust you with a $10,000 or a $100,000 mortgage loan? Once you established a good trust history, creditors are likely to offer you credit accounts. They will practically beg you to become their customer because of your credit history and score.

Your Credit Report aka credit history resumé.

This is a detailed document of all your past and present credit accounts. Your report also contains your address, phone number, place of employment, social security number, and current, derogatory and collection accounts. You do not have one credit report, you have three. They are Experian, Transunion, and Equifax. They update your account every 30 days if the creditor opts to pay their required fee. If your creditors does not report to the credit bureau, your new creditor will not know about your good or bad credit history.

Term of Loan

This is the amount of time it takes for you to pay the account off. An installment term is different from a revolving term. An installment term is the amount of time it takes for repayment. For example, you obtain a loan from a finance company for $1000 with a monthly repayment of $350 a month. The term of the loan is 12 months. This account is closed at the end of the term when you make your last payment. A revolving term is different from installment because you hold the power to say how long you want the account to stay open. The revolving loan does not close after you make your last payment. You can have this account open for a little as

2 days or as long as 20 years. You dictate the term of this account, unless you max out this account and make late payments. If this happens, the creditor will decide if it wants to close your account or decrease your credit limit.

What do you consider late payments?

Most people consider the account to be late after its due date or grace period has passed, which is technically late but you can be late without any of the credit bureaus being notified. If you have an unexpected expense and need to delay your car payment, most people would assume that since they are already 10 days late it's the same as being 35 days late WRONG! If you must make a late payment and you are comfortable paying a late fee (Giving away money), here's a secret:

Equifax, Transunion or Experian will never know unless you are 30 days late. Yep, you read correctly. Translation: If you are 29 days late paying your car loan you will probably pay an extra $50 late fee to your creditor, but you will not lose any credit points and your late payment will NOT be reported to the credit bureaus. Why? I'm glad you asked. The credit bureaus have their own system for reporting late payments. Which are 30days + 60days + 90days + 120days+; they only subtract credit points if you are 30, 60, 90 or 120 days late.

So, you can make your car payments 29 days late for the entire term of the loan, and it will not be on your credit report. However, I strongly advise against this.

For example, if the term of your car loan is 5 years, which is 60 months. 60 months x $50 = $3,000. Translation= you would pay an extra $3,000 in late payments added to your car loan in addition to your interest.

{ **A Monthly Payment is an agreement between the borrower and creditor of how much money would be paid to the creditor monthly.** }

- **Late Payment is any payment made after the original due date.**

* Don't forget a late payment will only show up on your credit report if it is more than 30 days late.*

• **Judgment is a decision made by the court from a lawsuit, in other words the court is mandating you to pay a debt.**

In relation to credit, it is common for creditors to sue clients for nonpayment of their debt. Some common accounts that normally file for a judgment are Bankruptcies, IRS debt Federal.

Terms to Remember

Late Payments are any payment made after the original due date.

Judgment is a decision made by the court from a lawsuit; in other words the court is mandating you to pay a debt.

Lien a is the right to keep or take possession of property belonging to someone else until the debt is paid in full or discharged.

Collections occur when a creditor sells the debt to a collecting agency so they can try to aggressively talk or threaten you into paying your debt.

Charge-Off is when the creditor reports to the credit bureaus that the debt is unlikely to be paid. The creditor typically reports the account as a charge-off after six to eight months of nonpayment.

Maxed -Out Credit Account is when your balance and limit are the same amount. If creditor give you an account with a limit of $300 and you spent $300. It will have a negative impact on your credit score.

Credit Report

Your credit history also known as a credit report consist of **five main factors and percentages**.

1) On-time payments – 35%

2) Capacity used (Percentage of credit used)- 30%

3) Length of credit history – 15%

4) Types of Credit used (Installment,

Revolving, Collections, Charge offs) – 10%

5) Past Credit Application (Inquires)-10%

CREDIT SCORE FACTORS

1. On-time Payment

It is imperative that you make your payments on time, it affects 35 percent of your total score. One late payment can cost you up to 80 points in as little as 30 days.

2. Capacity Used

Capacity Used, AKA balance versus limit. In other words, how much is your balance? Did you max out your account? If so, this will be a huge mistake. Why? I am glad you asked. A maxed-out account can do the same damage as one late payment. It can decrease your credit score by 100 points in 30 days. A maxed out credit card shows the creditor that you are an irresponsible credit card user.

3. Length of Credit History

Longevity is one major factor to increase to increase your score to 700 or 800 range. Credit history length is basically how long you have had a relationship with your creditors. Remember credit is based on trust. A creditor can't really trust you if you don't have a long history of keeping your accounts open and in good standing. It's not enough to pay an account on time for 1 or 2 years. Creditors love to see a revolving account that you have paid of time for 5 to 10 years with a low balance. You will have creditors calling, mailing, and begging you to open up an account with them.

4. Type of Credit Used (Revolving or Installment)

A revolving account is an account that does not close when you make your last payment with a balance of $0.00. Examples of revolving accounts are credit cards and store accounts (jewelry, clothing, furniture etc.) An installment account is a loan that you make monthly payments on. Once you make your last payment, that account is closed forever, never to reopen. You can open a new account with the same company, but you will have a new account number. Examples of installment accounts are automobile loans, mortgage loans, furniture loans, and personal and/or business loans. The key to remembering the difference between revolving verses and installment account is an installment account is a loan that the creditor paid a company so you could receive goods or service immediately and you (the borrower will pay the creditor monthly payments.) Furniture can actually be consider an installment or revolving account. The credit account depends on which finance company the furniture company decides to use to finance the furniture. Remember that an installment account is through a loan company (one account per purchase) with one account number. A revolving account is a credit account where you make multiple purchase with same account number.

5. Past Credit Application (Inquiries)

Inquiries can reduce your credit score extremely fast. For example, if you go to a car dealership and allow them to pull your credit for financing, and they can pull your credit at least 10 times, this inquiry can reduce your credit score by 20 to 50 points immediately.

Tips to Build or Rebuild your Credit

- Obtain credit.
- Obtain a Secured or Unsecured Credit Card.
- Make monthly payments on time.
- Get a loan from a bank rather than a small loan company.
- **Do Not** max out your credit account.
- **Do Not** obtain more than two new credit accounts when trying to build or rebuild your credit.

Activity

Obtain a copy of your credit report from each of the 3 major credit bureaus, and make a list of your credit history, separating the different items in the appropriate columns. A sample is listed in the first block. Karen Smith has an American Express credit card with a $10,000 credit limit that reports monthly to Equifax and Transunion. She has used 50% of her limit.

Creditor	Account Type	Limit	Balance	Credit Bureau EQ TU EX
American Express	Revolving	$10,000	$5,000	EQ, TU

Financial Literacy Made Easy

Creditor	Account Type	Limit	Balance	Credit Bureau EQ TU EX

To-Do List

Create a list of tasks you will complete to build or rebuild your credit based on the information you learned in the previous chapters.

1.
2.
3.
4.
5.
6.
7.
8.

9.

10.

11.

12.

13.

14.

15.

16.

17.

18.

19.

20.

Test your Knowledge

Let's see what you have learned as a result of reading this book! Answer the following questions based on your knowledge gained in each chapter, and assess how much you've grown in your knowledge of financial literacy as it relates to credit.

Part 1

True or False

1. Buy Here Pay Here accounts are some of the best accounts to rebuild your credit.

2. Equifax and Experian are two credit repair companies

3. A credit repair company can help you increase your credit score to 800.

4. Paying off your automobile loan can help me obtain good credit.

5. There are three major credit bureau: Equifax, Transunion and Experian.

6. I can obtain good credit by making my monthly mortgage payments.

7. Student loan accounts do not report late payments.

Multiple Choice Questions

1. Credit is

a.) money c.) buy now pay later
b.) an account d.) a, b, & c

2. My _____ should stay below 25% of my credit limit to help increase my credit scores.

    a.) debt to income ratio
    b.) credit score
    c.) credit card balance
    d.) inquiries

3. There are _____ major credit reporting agencies.

    a.) Two
    b.) three
    c.) five
    d.) one

4. What are inquiries?

    a.) new credit accounts

    b.) late payments

    c.) when a creditor looks at your credit report

    d.) derogatory accounts

5. You can order a **FREE** yearly credit report from

    a.) www.equifax.com

    b.) www.transunion.com

    c.) www.annualcreditreport.com

    d.) www.experian.com

6. If you are denied for a credit card you may want to apply for a _____ card.

a.) Master   c.) Visa

b.) Debit   d.) Secured

7. What is interest?

    a.) Taxes

    b.) late payment

    c.) the amount of money you pay back to creditor

    d.) the amount of time it takes to pay back a loan

Part 2

True or False

1. If I am trying to build my credit, I should open a personal loan account.

Financial Literacy Made Easy

2. An installment account is a contract that states when the account will close.

3. On-time payments will help me achieve an 800-credit score.

4. A 620-credit score is considered poor.

5. I must wait seven years after bankruptcy to purchase a home or automobile.

6. Bankruptcy accounts reports monthly to all three credit bureaus.

7. A maxed-out credit card does not hurt my credit scores if I

make my monthly payments on-time.

Multiple Choice Questions

1. An account with an end date is a (an)

    a.) revolving account

    b.) credit account

    c.) closed account

    d.) installment account

2. A relationship between a creditor and a customer that allows the customer to purchase items or services before payment is

    a.) Credit

    b.) capital

    c.) a customer

d.) interest

3. You are considered the _____, and the lender is the _____.

    a.) creditor, borrower

    b.) borrower, creditor

    c.) customer, borrower

    d.) borrower, bank

4. A _____ is a revolving account.

    a.) savings account

    b.) installment card

    c.) credit card

    d.) checking account

5. Which score is considered good credit?

    a.) 610- 670   c.) 760- 850

    b.) 611-below   d.) 680-759

6. Personal, automobile, and mortgage loans are _____.

    a.) installment accounts

    b.) credit accounts

    c.) bank accounts

    d.) revolving accounts

Answers

Part 1

True or False

1. False

2. False

3. False

4. False

5. True

6. False

7. False

Multiple Choice Questions

1. D

2. C

3. B

4. C

5. C

6. D

7. C

Part 2

True or False

1. False

2. True

3. False

4. False

5. False

6. False

7. False

Multiple Choice Questions

1. D

2. A

3. B

4. C

5. D

6. A

Glossary

Bad Credit: a score between 300 and 500 that makes the borrower have higher interest rates and less trust from creditors

Borrower: the person asking to receive an item, service, or money without paying in full

Charge Off: the status of an account when the creditor reports to the credit bureaus that the debt is unlikely to be paid

Collections: the status of an account when a creditor turns your account over or sells the debt to a collecting agency so they can try to aggressively talk you into paying your debt

Creditor: the business/entity you are asking to enter into a relationship with by applying for credit; lender

Credit Bureau: a collection agency that gathers account information from various creditors and provides that information to creditors concerning a borrower's credit history, i.e., Equifax, Transunion, and Experian

Credit Report: a collection of information recording a an individual's personal identification information (including previous and current addresses, employment information, social security number), past and current credit card accounts (numbers and types of accounts that are past due and in good standing), loans and repayment history (including late payment history), mortgages, the numbers and types of inquiries made into your credit history, bankruptcies, child support payment history, and statements of disputes.

Good Credit: a score between 650 and 700 that allows the borrower better interest rates and trust from creditors

Installment Account: an account that has a contract (binding agreement enforceable by law) with an established end date

Judgment: a decision made by the court from a lawsuit where the court is mandating you to pay a debt

Late Payments: any payment made after the original due date.

Lien: the right to keep or take possession of property belonging to someone else until the debt is paid in full or discharged

Middle Score: the credit score from one of the three credit bureaus used to determine lending capability, i.e., not the lowest or highest score, but the one in the middle

Revolving Account: an account that does not close when you make your last payment

ABOUT THE AUTHOR

Kesha Oliver Robinson is a native of Savannah, Georgia, a loving wife and mother, and a graduate of the Youth Challenge Academy, a nontraditional military school in Fort Stewart, Georgia. As a licensed realtor, member of the Savannah Board of Realtors, the National Association of Real Estate Brokers NARAB which it's local chapter is Savannah Association of Realtists, Robinson doesn't simply focus on the sale, she educates future home-buyers, guiding them through the process of achieving the American Dream. Her experience with down payment assistance programs for first time home-buyers like the Savannah Dream Maker and Georgia Dream, as well as the process of new construction makes Robinson stand out from the rest with rare knowledge and a caring heart.

This multitalented superwoman, who is also a licensed life, health and annuity agent, informs and inspires others to set attainable goals and work diligently toward achieving them. Her monthly, free financial literacy and home ownership workshops provide the community with valuable information and resources to create positive, wealth-building practices for generations to come. In addition to her monthly give back projects, Robinson also founded the community organization, My Sister's Keeper, Savannah. With the focus of mentoring, health awareness, and women's empowerment in multiple cities, this grassroots organization made a great impact on a great deal of individuals and families in the Southeast.

www.ingramcontent.com/pod-product-compliance
Lightning Source LLC
Chambersburg PA
CBHW070318230526
45470CB00002B/932